Ivan Strebel

Mobile Computing & Application Stores

GRIN Verlag

Bibliografische Information der Deutschen Nationalbibliothek:

Die Deutsche Bibliothek verzeichnet diese Publikation in der Deutschen National-
bibliografie; detaillierte bibliografische Daten sind im Internet über http://dnb.d-
nb.de/ abrufbar.

Impressum:

Copyright © 2011 GRIN Verlag GmbH
Druck und Bindung: Books on Demand GmbH, Norderstedt Germany
ISBN: 978-3-656-09396-1

Dieses Buch bei GRIN:

http://www.grin.com/de/e-book/184594/mobile-computing-application-stores

GRIN - Your knowledge has value

Der GRIN Verlag publiziert seit 1998 wissenschaftliche Arbeiten von Studenten, Hochschullehrern und anderen Akademikern als eBook und gedrucktes Buch. Die Verlagswebsite www.grin.com ist die ideale Plattform zur Veröffentlichung von Hausarbeiten, Abschlussarbeiten, wissenschaftlichen Aufsätzen, Dissertationen und Fachbüchern.

Besuchen Sie uns im Internet:

http://www.grin.com/

http://www.facebook.com/grincom

http://www.twitter.com/grin_com

Mobile Computing & Application Stores
Trabajo Tecnologías Emergentes - Telemática

Ivan Strebel

Especialización en Sistemas de Información
Universidad EAFIT, Medellín – Colombia

ABSTRACT

Due to technological developments in mobile devices and wireless technlogies, mobile applications are conquering the world these days. In this work, we will first have a look at the specific features, advantages and existing categories of such applications. Secondly, the emergence of application stores, their characteristics and the according changes in the distribution process of mobile applications will be presented. Finally, the strengths, weaknesses and features of mobile banking will be described and possible ways to improve the adaption of mobile banking applications will be discussed.

Content

1. Introduction

The rapid growth of mobile applications in the recent years is closely related to the appearance and widespread use of smartphones and tablet computers. The emergence of these new technologies also triggers important changes in the market for mobile applications, shifting the market power from classic providers away to now market players. The convergence of Internet, mobile devices and wireless technologies also opened the way for mobile banking a s an innovative method for accessing banking services via mobile devices.

In this work, in chapter 2, a brief introduction into mobile applications, their features and advantages will be given. In chapter 3, a closer look will be taken on the application stores and their characteristics. Furthermore the changes, which are occurring in the market-structure due to the appearance of these application stores, will be described.
Chapter 4 is entirely dedicated to the subject of mobile banking. Strengths and weaknesses of this special field for mobile applications will be shown and reasons identified why mobile banking still remains in its infancy. Furthermore some indications will be given, to which features a mobile banking provider must pay attention to be successful. Finally some concluding remarks summarize the gained insights of this work.

2. Mobile Applications

2.1 Mobile applications overview

Mobile applications are a rapidly growing and developing segment of the global market for mobile devices. Basically, they consist of software that runs on a mobile device and performs certain tasks for the user. Mobile computing had reached the research community quite some time ago and finally has found now they way to the commercial industry and mainstream users through PDAs and smartphones. The constant technological improvement in hardware, processing power and wireless network bandwidth further enhances the capabilities of mobile devices and at the same time increases the use of mobile applications. More than ever, mobile devices can run rich stand-alone applications as well as distributed client-server applications that information via web gateways.

For many years, the development of mobile services had been mostly under the control of network operators, phone manufacturers and content providers. This market structure has recently changed with the arrival of software companies with new mobile phones and platforms such as iPhone and Android. This shake-up led to an important changes in the market structure where the roles are now changing. Some actors are loosing control of certain aspects of the value chain (i.e. mobile network operators) and some new actors are generating revenue streams (i.e. portal providers) [Holzer and Ondrus, 2011].

2.2 Mobile application specific features and advantages

Mobile applications are characterized by some unique features, which equip them with certain advantages over conventional applications [Tiwari and Buse, 2007]:

2.2.1 Features:

1. Ubiquity:

   Ubiquity means that the user can avail of services and carry out transactions largely independent of his current geographic location ("anywhere" feature). This makes it possible to offer location-based services, which are specific to a given context.

2. Immediacy:

   Closely related to the feature of ubiquity is the possibility of real-time availment of services ("anytime" feature). This feature is particularly attractive for services that are time-critical and demand a fast reaction, e.g. stock market information for a broker. Additionally, the consumer can buy goods and services, as and when he feels the need. The immediacy of transaction helps to capture consumers at the moment of intention so that sales are not lost in the discrepancy between the point of intention and that of the actual purchase.

3. Localisation:

Positioning technologies, such as the Global Positioning System (GPS), allow companies to offer goods and services to the user specific to his current location. Location based services can be, thus, offered to meet consumers' needs and wishes for localised content and services.

4. Instant connectivity:

Ever since the introduction of the General Packet Radio Service (GPRS) mobile devices are constantly "online", i.e. in touch with the network ("always-on" feature). This feature brings convenience to the user, as time-consuming dial-up or boot processes are not necessary.

5. Pro-active functionality:

Mobile Applications opens, by the virtue of its ability to be immediate, local and personal, new avenues for push-marketing, such as content- and product offers. Services like "Opt-in advertising" can be offered, so that a user may choose the products, services and companies which he wants to be kept informed about. The Short Message Service (SMS) can be used to send brief text messages to consumers informing them of relevant local offerings that best suit their needs. This feature ensures that the "right" (relevant) information can be provided to the user at the "right" place, at the "right" time. On the other hand, the user does not have to fear missing some potentially crucial information or getting it too late.

6. Simple authentication procedure:

Mobile telecommunication devices function with an electronic chip called Subscriber Identity Module (SIM). The SIM is registered with the network operator and the owner is thus unambiguously identifiable. The clear identification of the user in combination with an individual Personal Identification Number (PIN) makes any further time-consuming, complicated and potentially inefficient authentication process redundant.

These unique features of Mobile Commerce can provide the user with the following concrete and specific advantages:

1. Context-specific services:

Mobile Commerce makes it possible to offer location based services, which are specific to a given context (e.g. time of the day, location and the interests of the user). Such services offer new opportunities for personalised push-marketing in close proximity to the vendor thereby increasing the probability of sales. It enhances brand presence and thus encourages consumers to remain loyal to brands they are acquainted with.

2. Time-critical situations:

The ubiquity and immediacy of Mobile Applications allow the user to perform urgent tasks in an efficient manner, e.g. fast reaction to stock market developments irrespective of his current geographic location. It is also useful in emergency situations.

3. Spontaneous decisions and needs:
   Spontaneous needs are not externally triggered and generally involve decisions that do not require a very careful consideration, e.g. purchase decisions involving small amounts of money. An example of such a service would be reserving a place in a restaurant or cinema spontaneously. Users may also be provided with access to entertainment content, e.g. horoscope, music or sport news while on the move and with free time on the hand.

4. Efficiency increase:
   Mobile Commerce helps increase the productivity of the workforce by increasing the efficiency of their daily routines. Time-pressured consumers (employees) can use 'dead spots' in the day, e.g. during the daily travel to and from workplace, more effectively. This can be utilised, e.g. to check e-mails, get current news, order products and carry out bank transactions.

2.3 Mobile application categories

Today available technologies make it possible to offer a wide range of mobile services to users. The can be bundled into the following main categories [Tiwari and Buse, 2007; Mobile Marketing Association, 2008]:

Mobile Application Categories	
Application Category	**Examples**
Mobile Communication	- Email - Chats - Social Networks
Mobile Information Services	- News - Travel information - Weather - Currency Converter - GPS and location services - Translators - Itineraries - Search Engines
Mobile Entertainment	- Video Players - Audio Players - Live Streaming - Games
Mobile Banking	- Mobile Accounting - Mobile Brokerage - Financial Information
Mobile Productivity	- Calendars - Calculators - Spreadsheets - Mobile Office - Address Book
Mobile Shopping	- Purchasing of goods and services
Mobile Ticketing	- Public Transport - Sports- and Cultural Events - Check-In

	- Mobile Parking
Mobile Telematic Services	- Navigation Services - Remote diagnosis - Vehicle Tracking - Emergency Services

3. Application Stores

3.1 A new player in the market

The market mechanism fort he distribution of mobile applications, as mentioned before, has changed drastically in the last couple of years. In this section we will take a closer look at the application stores that have been surging as new players in the distribution process.

Basically, the distribution process consists of three main elements as shown in Figure 1 [Holzer and Ondrus, 2011]:

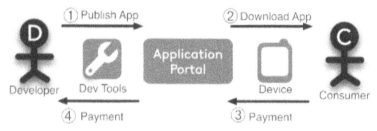

Figure 1. Mobile application distribution process.

First, the developer uses development tools to build its mobile application. Second, the developer publishes its application on a portal, from which the consumer can download the application onto its mobile device. In this model, the application portal plays an intermediary role between the service provider and the customer. This approach is different from the model in place until recently, where mobile network operators where in charge of being the interface between customers and service providers.

3.2 Two-sided market

The application stores are part of typical two-sided market where an increase or decrease on one side of the market induces a similar effect on the other side of the market. In other words, if the number of consumers increases for a given platform, application store or mobile device, the number of developers attracted to this platform, application store or mobile device will also increase. Similarly, as the number of developers, and thus the number of applications increase, the platform, portal, or mobile device will attract even more consumers. So on the one hand, developers have an incentive to develop for the most popular mobile devices using the most popular platform, and to publish their applications on the most popular portal in order to reach the largest number of consumers. On the other hand, consumers have an incentive to buy devices running a platform with many applications. This mechanism creates a positive feedback loop, as depicted in Figure 2.

In order to trigger this positive feedback loop in typical two-sided markets, producers tend to bring enhancing products to the customers at very low, or even loss-making prices (e.g. Videogame consoles, credit cards). This behaviour can now also be observed in the market for mobile applications (e.g. Kindle Fire).

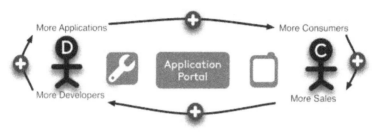

Figure 2. Positive feedback loop in the two-sided mobile application market.

3.3 Characteristics of Application stores

Holzer and Ondrus (2011) mention several characteristics of Application Stores from which some will be described in this section:

No storage cost:
As there is no storage cost, portals can generate revenues not only from their best selling applications but also from a plethora of applications only sold a few times. This is especially relevant as there is no extra cost in carrying such lame-duck applications. It is expected, that the amount of such low-selling applications will grow with the number of developers attracted to the portal. This feature is especially interesting from the point of view of the variety and diversity of applications that is expected to evolve.

Centralized versus decentralized stores:
With a decentralized portal, developers can freely upload and distribute their applications on any third-party portal, as there is no centralized policy. In this model, all portal providers compete in order to attract customers and applications. The downside for the consumer is that the great variety of portals does not provide a comprehensive overview of existing applications. An advantage for platform providers is that there is no need to put in place and maintain a centralized solution. The application market is handed over to third parties. Players such as Nokia, Microsoft, and LiMo have mostly used a decentralized portal approach so far.

In the centralized model, one portal is proposed as the main portal on which all applications are published. This approach gives the main portal provider a competitive advantage over others. Consumers can easily find and download applications. It also facilitates the job of developers by offering a single point of sale. Centralized portals can benefit from network effects by attracting more consumers and more developers. Apple and Google propose a single point of sale with the AppStore and the Android Market.

However, these two platforms have different approaches. On the one hand, Apple pushes a unique and exclusive portal with a strict application review process. Google, on the other hand, does not restrict the publication of applications to its portal. Moreover, there are no plans to review applications prior to publication as it counts on consumers' feedback to exclude inappropriate and low-quality applications.

Recently, other platforms like Nokia, RIM and Microsoft are also moving in the direction of a centralized application store (Figure 3).

Figure 3. Portal Trends

Device uniformity versus device variety:
Application stores can choose to target only one or a few devices with similar technical features. This approach allows platform providers to have an extensive control on devices and standardized features. Moreover, operation systems can be more easily fine-tuned to the uniform devices. The main drawbacks reside in a strong reliance on the device manufacturer and possibly a smaller user base. A good illustration of this strategy is Apple which offers its OS only to a few relatively similar mobile devices (iPhone, iPad and iPod Touch). This strategy enhances standardization of the devices and lower dependence on various device manufacturers (e.g., Samsung, LG, Motorola). The platform provider has more control on the devices and lower compatibility issues of its operation system.

Platforms can chose to allow their operation system to run on a variety of mobile phones manufactured by different vendors. Through this strategy, platforms can reach more potential customers. This approach also allows to be less dependent on individual manufacturers; the pressure is on manufacturers rather than on the platform when it comes to prices and features. The main drawback is the customization for the specifications of different devices and different manufacturers. Currently all platform providers, except Apple, follow this approach.

Commercial platforms were traditionally targeting a variety of devices. Apple and Google both began by targeting uniform devices. However, Google shifted its approach to target different devices and manufacturers, leaving Apple alone in the uniform category as depicted in Figure 4.

① Diverse Devices

② Uniform Devices

Figure 4. Device Set

4. Mobile Banking

4.1 Overview

In general, Mobile Banking refers to the provision and availment of banking- and financial services with the help of mobile telecommunication devices. According to Tiwari and Buse (2007), there are 3 important aspects, in which Mobile Banking can create utility to a bank:

1. Mobile Banking as Distribution Channel:
   Mobile Banking enhances the number of existing channels of distribution that a bank employs to offer its services. The term 'distribution channel' hereby signifies a medium of delivery that a vendor employs to deliver his products or services to customers.

2. Mobile banking as Image Product:
   The bank may hope to win or retain a positive image amongst technology-savvy sections of the society and strengthen the brand-reputation of being innovative and visionary. The image of being a technology leader can help the bank win customers who are looking for modern products and services and at the same time help it retain its own existing base of technology-savvy customers, some of whom otherwise might have switched to other banks while looking for such a product.

3. Mobile Banking as Source of Revenue:
   Apart from functioning as an additional distribution channel Mobile Banking can also serve as a source of revenue. Mobile services can be offered on a premium basis. The price, in this case, should be reasonable enough so that customers are willing to pay them but at the same time they should be – from a financial point of view – higher than the costs incurred by the bank.

As any mobile application, mobile banking offers a wide range of potential benefits to its users (as mentioned before). From the point of view of a bank, the following strengths can be outlined:

1. Increasing Sales Volume:
One of the primary tasks of a distribution channel is to increase the volume of demand for products at profitable prices. This objective is achieved by increasing operational efficiency so that those losses in the sales are minimised. Mobile Banking can contribute to achieve this goal by following means:
    1. Anytime, anywhere access to banking services;
    2. Availability of push services to suggest transactions on an urgent basis.
    3. Face-to-face talks with the personal consultant via video telephony.

2. Reducing costs of distribution:
In times of increased competition, a distribution channel must organise business processes efficiently so as to reduce distribution costs. Mobile Banking can contribute to achieve this goal by following means:

1. The manual collection, processing, transmission and archiving of data by bank employees in branch offices is substituted, as in the Internet- based banking, by automated processes.

2. As against Internet Banking, Mobile Banking makes it possible to offer ubiquitous, semi-personal consulting services in real time. These services can be centralised to exploit economies of scale and scope as well as regional cost differences.

3. Diversification of distribution channels helps reduce the business costs that arise in the form of sales lost due to sudden collapse of a channel and to minimise customer dissatisfaction.

3. Increasing customer satisfaction
Mobile Banking may help a bank increase the customer satisfaction ratio by adopting the following means:

1. Streamlining of business processes to increase efficiency;

2. More attention and better consulting for individual customers due to automation of routine processes

3. Innovative "anywhere, anytime" services customised for individual preferences and the current geographic location of the customer provide value-added to the customer.

4. The collected data can be utilised to create customer profiles.

Mobile banking still remains in its infancy although is perceived as one of the most significant technological innovations concerning mobile devices. Two main reasons for this phenomenon are mentioned [Kun and Namho, 2009]:

Technical limitations
One of the reasons why international mobile banking usage rates have remained fairly low has to do with the technical limitations these systems face. The customer experience using small screens and keypads and slower transaction speeds is clearly inferior, especially if compared to internet banking.

Trust in security
Even though mobile banking technologies are available for quite some time now, the user's distrust in wireless transactions has hampered the widespread adoption of mobile banking systems.

4.3 Importance and future evolution of mobile banking
Different survey results [Tiwari and Buse, 2007] have demonstrated unambiguously that Mobile Banking has staged a remarkable comeback. Whereas most banks and indeed many experts believed Mobile Banking to be dead after the dotcom burst, banks are seeing themselves increasingly forced to include mobile services in their product portfolios. The reasons for this extraordinary resurrection are:

- The phenomenal growth of the telecommunication sector and the resultant (unparalleled) penetration of the society by mobile phones present unique business opportunities for protagonists in the market.

- A new generation of technology- and innovation friendly consumers is taking over the centre stage in business- and social life of the society. This generation is more open to the opportunities presented by mobile telecommunication.

The ongoing process of globalisation and the integration of the world-economy are forcing working professionals to be on the move within national and international geographic boundaries. These professionals need to carry out their bank business also while on the move even when they do not necessarily have access to an Internet-capable computer. The "anytime, anywhere" feature of Mobile Banking is thus nothing less than a professional necessity for many of them (Figure 5).

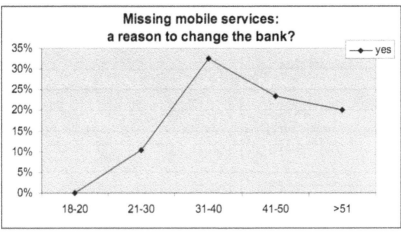

Figure 5. Willingness across age-groups to change bank for Mobile Banking

Therefore, the worldwide number of mobile banking users is expected to grow from 55 million users in 2009 to 894 million users in 2015 (Cano and Domenech-Asensi, 2011). Additionally, as phones become more sophisticated, it is expected, that they will begin replacing computers as consumer's preferred device for accessing the internet. In China for example, 29% of internet users have no access to computers and access the web via mobile handsets (Card Technology Today, 2009).

4.4 Technologies

Mobile Banking services should fulfil certain safety criteria in order to ensure customer acceptance as well as business viability [Tiwari and Buse, 2007]:

1. Confidentiality: The data must be protected in a way that prohibits any unauthorised access from taking place.

2. Authentication: Access to data may be granted only when the user identity has been ascertained and authenticated.

3. Integrity: Encryption techniques must be employed to avoid manipulation of the data during transmission. The bank and the customer, both, should be able to verify the integrity of the transmitted data by cross-checking the validity of certain pre-stipulated attributes.

4. Non-disputability: Transactions must be documented, e.g. by generating detailed log files and preserving them for a reasonably long time to allow the customer to take note of the transaction and to report discrepancies, if any, to the bank. So that the non-disputability of customer instructions can be ensured, if needed before a court of law.

In order to meet these data protection/safety standards, Applications based on three different types of technologies are being used [Tiwari and Buse, 2007]:

Browser-based Applications

Browser-based applications generate the user interface on the server and transport it subsequently to the mobile device. This interface is then presented to the user graphically with the help of a browser. The main advantage of a browser-based application is that data-processing is conducted solely on and by the server. There is, thus, no requirement for the presence of additional software or of significant processing power on the mobile device. Browser-based applications are hence suitable for mobile devices with low memory- or processing power, e.g. mobile phones

Messaging-based Applications

In messaging-based applications the communication between the bank and the customer is carried out via text messages. These messages may be triggered automatically by the bank, whenever certain predefined events occur, for instance whenever a transaction is performed on the account. Alternatively, the messages may be sent by the bank as a response/confirmation to customer requests. A customer message may contain either an instruction, e.g. to carry out a transaction, or an information request, e.g. for the account status.

Client-based Applications

Client-based Mobile Banking applications are those, which require software to be installed on the mobile device. Transactions can be prepared offline (e.g. entry of necessary details). Once all necessary data have been keyed in, a connection to the server is established and the data transmitted. Before the data is transmitted a security check takes place by means of PIN and TAN. Client-based applications are attractive because a significant part of banking process is conducted offline reducing online connection time and costs.

4.5 Acceptance of Mobile Banking and generation of trust

As already mentioned before in chapter 4.2.2, one of the main limitations for the widespread acceptance of mobile banking is the lack of trust in the security of the technology. Therefore, any company that considers offering mobile services must take into account ways how to transmit the perception of secure mobile services to it's customers. Two studies investigating the concept of trust [Tiwari and Buse, 2007; Meridea, 2003] found clear indicators, that the main disadvantage mobile banking suffers, is the user's concern towards security (Figure 6). This is especially true regarding services that include transactions (Figure 7).

Disadvantage	Meridea (2003)	Uni Hamburg (2005)
Security Concerns	31%	77%
Costs Issues (too expensive)	12%	44%
Complicated / Uncomfortable Usage	4%	30%

Figure 6. Customer Acceptance of Mobile Banking

Service	Meridea (2003)	Uni Hamburg (2005)
Balance Enquiry	98%	78%
Transaction Thresholds	95%	44%
Card Management	90%	78%
Mobile Brokerage Transactions	40%	33%

Figure 7. Comparison of user perception of disadvantages

4.5.1 Recommendations

Several groups of researchers have investigated the ways of how trust towards mobile banking can be increased. Some of their findings will be briefly discussed here [Lin, 2011; Kun and Namho, 2009].

System- and information quality:
Factors that enable stability and accuracy of the mobile banking system as well as the provision of accurate information for conducting mobile transactions are important to create customer's trust in mobile banking.

Usefulness and easy-to-use:
Perceived relative advantage and ease of use were observed to have significant effects on adopting mobile banking. Moreover, customer perceptions about the compatibility with their values, experiences, preferences and lifestyle appear to be a good predictor of adoption of mobile banking.
The design quality of the offered service surprisingly seems to have no influence on customer satisfaction.

Competence of the service provider:
If customers believe, the mobile banking firm is able to develop effective services and provide adequate protection from fraud, then adaption intentions increase.

4.6 Demography

Mobile banking adopters seem to show different socio-demographic characteristics [Luo et al., 2010]. Adopters are relatively young, with the majority in the age group of 24-34. They are mostly white-collar workers and students with average income levels.

Tiwari and Buse, (2007) suggest to adapt the offered services in mobile banking to three core target groups to better fulfil their corresponding needs:

The Youngsters:
The segment of 14–18 years old youth has acquired an important role in the growth of mobile telecommunications and related services. This group is reported to be technology-savvy and willing to experiment with innovative products and services. The youngsters, often on the move, demand ubiquitous, anytime service. Though the youngsters as a group are hardly relevant for banks from a financial perspective, they

represent the prospective clientele of tomorrow and need to be cultivated in the middle to long-term marketing strategy of the banks.

The Young Adults:
Also this segment is thought to be technology- and innovation friendly. Though this group is financially not very strong either, many members of this group are known to be involved in stock market activities and are increasingly attractive for banks. Further, this group can be expected to enter in short to middle-run a professional carrier so that it needs to be cultivated in order to retain customers of this age-group once they enter professional lives.

The Business People:
This group of customers, generally in the age- group of 25–36 years, is thought to be the most important one for Mobile Banking. Members of this group are generally well educated and economically well-off. They need to be often on the move for professional reasons. Therefore, they carry mobile devices to ensure accessibility. For this reason they are ideal candidates to use services offered via mobile devices. From the banks' perspective this group is particularly attractive on account of its relative economic prosperity and the need for financial services, e.g. home loans for young families. Such a group of customers is generally looking forward to do business with known and trusted brands that simultaneously offer individual advisory services.

4.7 Specific Products and Services
In general, mobile banking offers the following services: Financial information services, mobile accounting , mobile brokerage and mobile payment. In this section they will be described briefly.

4.7.1 Mobile Payment:
The term "Mobile Payment" refers to payments that are made via mobile hand-held devices in order to purchase goods and services. Mobile Payment services usually act as intermediary between consumer and vendor.

4.7.2 Mobile Accounting:
Mobile Accounting are banking services that revolve around a standard bank account and are conducted and/or availed by mobile devices. Mobile Accounting services may be divided in two categories to differentiate between services that are essential to operate an account and services that are essential to administer an account (Figure 8).

Mobile Accounting	
Account Operation	Account Administration
Money remittances & transfers	Access administration
Standing orders for bill payments	Changing operative accounts
Money transfer to sub-accounts	Blocking lost cards
Subscribing insurance policies	Cheque book requests

Figure 8. Services in Mobile Accounting

4.7.3 Mobile Brokerage:

Brokerage, in the context of banking- and financial services, refers to intermediary services related to the stock exchange centre, e.g. sell and purchase of stocks, bonds, funds, derivatives and foreign exchange among others. Mobile Brokerage, thus, refers to mobile financial services of non-informational nature revolving around a securities account.

Mobile Brokerage, too, may be divided in two categories to differentiate between services that are essential to operate a securities account and services that are essential to administer that account (Figure 9). As is the case with Mobile Accounting, Mobile Brokerage requires informational services in order to facilitate brokerage activities. For this reason, Mobile Brokerage is invariably offered in combination with services related to Mobile Financial Information.

Mobile Brokerage	
Account Operation	Account Administration
Selling & purchasing financial instruments (e.g. securities)	Access administration
	Order book administration

Figure 9. Services in Mobile Brokerage

4.7.4 Mobile Financial Information Services

Mobile Financial Information refers to non-transaction based banking- and financial services of informational nature. Mobile Financial Information services include subsets from both banking and financial services and are meant to provide the customer with anytime, anywhere access to information. The information may either concern the bank and securities accounts of the customer or it may be regarding market developments with relevance for that individual customer. This sub-application may also be divided into two categories:

Mobile Financial Information	
Account Information	**Market Information**
Balance inquiries / Latest transactions	Foreign exchange rates
Statement requests	Market and bank-specific interest rates
Threshold alerts	Commodity prices
Returned cheques / cheque status	Stock market quotes and reports
Credit card information	Product information & offers
Branches and ATM locations	–
Helpline and emergency contact	–
Information on the completion status	–

Figure 10. Services in Mobile Financial Information

5. Conclusion

The constant development and convergence of information technologies such as mobile devices, wireless technologies and internet in the recent years have led to a boom in the development and use of mobile applications. These mobile applications possess some unique features, which equip them with certain advantages over conventional applications and led to a broad range of different purposes for which these are being used.

The widespread use of smartphones and PDAs has also led to a profound change in the distribution process of mobile applications. Whereas mobile network providers and phone manufacturers used to be the main actors in the market, nowadays there position has been taken by application stores. These new market players open up new opportunities for customers and developers of mobile applications. Currently, different models of application stores exist and it has to be seen whether all of them will remain in their actual business model.

Mobile banking, until now, has failed to reach significant number of users and still remains in its infancy. Although such applications offer a wide range of advantages to customers and banks, adoption rates have remained low. This is mainly attributed to a lack of trust of the customers in the available technology and the technical limitations of mobile devices. Recent technological developments, globalisation and a change of habits of bank customers seem to inevitably change this trend. As for most innovative technologies, the critical success factors in its implementation strategy lies within the appropriate adaption of offered service to core target groups.

The pace in which the use of mobile applications has spread in the recent years has seen a drastic increase. This trend probably is irreversible and the ways in which mobile applications will influence our lives is multiplying. Therefore it is probable, that the use of mobile banking and application stores will become as normal as it is the use of email today but still remains to be seen.

6. References

Cano, Maria-Dolores and Domenech-Asensi, Gines (2011). A secure energy-efficient m-banking application for mobile devices. *The Journal of Systems and Software*, 04: 1899-1909

Challenges, but opportunities for mobile banking (2009). *Card Technology Today*, 21;4: 5-6

Holzer, Adrian and Ondrus, Jan (2011). Mobile application market: A developer's perspective. *Telematics and Informatics,* 28: 22-31

Kun, Chang Lee and Namho, Chung (2009). Understanding factors affecting trust in and satisfaction with mobile banking in Korea: A modified DeLone and McLean's model perspective. *Interacting with Computers*, 21: 385-392

Lin, Hsiu-Fen (2011). An empirical investigation of mobile banking adoption: The effect of innovation attributes and knowledge-based trust. *International Journal of Information Management,* 31: 252-260

Luo, Xin; Li, Han; Zhang, Jie and Shim J.P. (2010). Examining multi-dimensional trust and multi-faceted risk in initial acceptance of emerging technologies: An empirical study of mobile banking services. *Decision Support Systems*, 49: 222-234

Meridea (2003). *Ergebnisse einer Befragung von privaten Bankkunden zum Thema Mobile Banking*, Helsinki.

Mobile Marketing Association (2008). Mobile Applications. *www.mmaglobal.com*

Tiwari, Rajnish and Buse, Stephan (2007). The Mobile Commerce Prospects: A Strategic Analysis of Opportunities in the Banking Sector. *Hamburg University Press*